Silences

Gulzar was born in Dina (now in Pakistan) in 1934. After the partition of India, he lived in Delhi. The world of Indian films lured the poet and songwriter to Bombay, where he worked as assistant to some distinguished directors like Bimal Roy and Hrishikesh Mukherjee. He has written stories for more than fifty films, and numerous songs. He has directed some memorable movies such as *Mere Apne*, *Achanak*, *Aandhi*, *Mausam*, *Khushboo*, *Kinara*, *Meera*, *Koshish*, *Ijaazat*, *Parichay*, *Kitaab*, *Lekin* and *Maachis*. He has made two television serials—*Mirza Ghalib* and *Kirdaar*, several documentaries and has published three volumes of poetry.

Rina Singh was born in India and settled in Canada in 1980. She is the author of *Selected Poems* (Writer's Workshop, Kolkata). Her poems and stories have appeared in several Canadian literary journals. She has a master's degree in creative writing from Concordia University, Montreal, and a teaching degree from McGill University, Montreal, where she taught creative writing for several years. She is also an artist and has exhibited oil paintings in Montreal. At present she teaches in Toronto, where she lives with her husband and two children.

Silences
Selected Poems

Gulzar

Translated by

Rina Singh

RUPA

Published by
Rupa Publications India Pvt. Ltd 2013
7/16, Ansari Road, Daryaganj
New Delhi 110002

Sales centres:
Allahabad Bengaluru Chennai
Hyderabad Jaipur Kathmandu
Kolkata Mumbai

ISBN: 978-81-291-2030-4

10 9 8 7 6 5 4 3 2 1

The moral right of the author has been asserted.

Typeset in Footlight by Mindways Design, New Delhi

Printed at Repro Knowledgecast Limited, India

For Bosky

I didn't see time come
I didn't see time go
I didn't see time passing by
I didn't see any divine face
discard it

but I saw time
collect it in one place;

maybe it tiptoed from dreams
but when it came
even the thoughts didn't notice.
I saw the colour in the
eyes deepen like the sunset
I kissed it
but I didn't recognise it.

I think I heard it in lisping words;
I saw my baby
wrapped in silken threads
I had no idea
that it was time wrapped there.

I searched for it
in the growing fingernails,
in bracelets,
in books,
I had no idea that it was time written there.

I didn't see time come
I didn't see time go
I didn't even see it passing by

but I saw time collect in one place—
this year Bosky will turn eighteen.

Gulzar

For Pinks

—Rina Singh

Contents

Preface

Silences is an echo of my voice.

There is always an inherent silence in a poem. The poet hides behind that silence and yet he is loud enough to be echoed by those who share his heartbeats.

Rina chose this title, for she thought my silence is more eloquent than my voice.

I must confess that I have always carried a sort of unsure feeling about my poems. At times I felt they are good; while at other times I was not so sure. When Rina sent me her translations, I felt quite reassured. I wrote back to Rina that I knew my poems were good, but I didn't know they were beautiful too. Rina has correctly heard the whispers of words and their silent meanings. I have always felt that words are not solid blocks of meaning. They say much more than their apparent shapes. It was very satisfying when my daughter Meghna (Bosky) started sharing my poems, who had never quite followed the Urdu idiom.

Reading my poems in English is like seeing them in a new dress; well stitched, well starched and ironed very carefully. When I used to read my poems in Urdu, they used to sound like me. In English they sound like my teachers. I used to like them. Now I am impressed by them.

I can't explain anything more about my poems than what a poem explains for itself. I think there is a feel about them. If I explain they will cease to be poems.

Gulzar

Translating Gulzar

It is difficult to draw a 'profile' of Gulzar and I shall not attempt it. His talents are manifold and his achievements voluminous. His poetry should be allowed to speak for him because there is no better way of knowing a person than through what he writes. Gulzar is better known as a film-maker and for those who see only his 'worldly' success will probably fail to grasp the meaning of his sadness and the 'unworldliness' of his poetry.

The Indian film world which he has chosen as his milieu is such that it calls for a very tough hide indeed. His poetry reveals that he has not only failed to develop such a hide but remained more thin-skinned than most people.

A sensitivity like his, a ruthless environment like his can make life very painful. While translating his poetry, I have felt his pain and witnessed a great spiritual distress.

Wandering in a dark barren world, a world crazed with violent, roaring sounds, this poet carries a lump of silence in his throat. The poet in him panics by the sorrows of life and says to him:

Come let's commit suicide!

The thought of suicide is not strange to Gulzar. He witnesses his own death almost with fascination. But the silence in him lets him overcome the temptation and reaffirms his faith in life because:

Suicide is a darkness not a solution.

Suicide can be a temptation to conquer loneliness but like Dag Hammarskjold he too believes that "Death is to be your final gift to Life, but it must not be an act of treachery against it". Gulzar, in one of his poems, says:

Remember not to disfigure the face of Death
with any wrinkle of Life

The agony in his poetry can only be felt, not translated.

When some people began to ask me why I chose Gulzar, I mentioned it to him and asked him as to what I should say. He jokingly said to me: "Tell them you made a mistake and now you want everyone to know."

But it was by no mistake that I chose Gulzar for this literary endeavour. I first met him in 1980 and he gave me his then newly published book, *Kuch Aur Nazme*, and I have been in love with his poetry ever since. Perhaps it is his experience of pain, loneliness and alienation that has struck a sympathetic chord within me.

It was only last year that I met him again and showed him some of the translations. His response was so encouraging and inspiring that I not only began to take my translations seriously, I began to write poetry after many years.

Gulzar wrote to me after receiving my translations:

"I have never felt so excited about my own poems, as I did today after reading your translations. So far they were just lying there.

For the first time somebody picked them up, wiped them, cleaned their faces and presented them to me."

It felt great that the end product was accepted so warmly but to me the process itself has been a beautiful experience.

Translation in a way is a difficult task. A translator does not have too much freedom to be creative. But what Yevtushenko once said about poetry translation gave me courage to take more risks without in any way taking from the original.

He said: "Poetry translation is like a woman; if it's beautiful it's not faithful and if it's faithful it's not beautiful."

The task of translation is difficult also because to put any kind of intensity into another person's work, you have to feel with your whole being. Somehow I found an unexplainable rapport with his poetry. If the translations have any merit it is because I have felt each poem filter through my soul and I would like to consider it a little tribute to a great poet and a gentle, lovable person.

Although Gulzar's talents are manifold—he is a renowned film-maker, known for films that are unique, a story writer, a dialogue writer, a lyricist of hauntingly beautiful songs—poetry remains a single overwhelming talent and passion that colours all his other talents and probably defines his function on earth.

Rina Singh

rain

When it rains
water grows feet,
kicking against walls
in the street
jumping
like a bunch of boys
after winning a match.

After winning the match
the boys of the street
with canvas shoes
jump like balls
kicking against walls
in the street
jumping
like water
when it rains.

communal riots

No man was hacked in the city;
those were only names
that were murdered.

Nobody beheaded anyone;
only the severed hats
had heads in them.

And the blood
you see on the streets
belongs to the butchered voices.

light

Stars in the sky,
sparks in the eyes,
greasy patches of light
stain my vision.
The pointed light
pokes my eyelids,
hurts my eyes.

Lead me and put me back
in the lap of velvety darkness;
compress the gauze
of pitch darkness
on my eyes:

this burning lava of light
is blinding me.

empty box

An empty box
opened,
knifed,
beating against walls
lying uselessly
on the streets.

Flattened out
rolling along
meaninglessly.

Just like this day
empty
blank
so utterly useless.

twin

This poet who was born with me
has poured
the sands of moonlight
in my heart
flung at my eyes
the choicest pains of life.

Clenching my soul
between his teeth
he has scraped the burning wounds
of my breath
and burnt my shoulders, always
saying "Pain brings realization."

Now panicked
by his own sorrow
says to me: "Come
let's commit suicide."

paper boat

From the crossing
to the market
from the market
to the street
the paper boat
in monsoon's
orphaned waters
uncertain
unsure
asks:
Every boat finds a shore
where is mine?

How cruel
of some innocent child
to have given meaning
to a meaningless
piece of paper.

déjà vu

I wonder what it was that
I wanted to say to you today!

I met you and I forget
what I said
what I had thought I'd say,
when I met you
I had this feeling
I have already said it to you.

There are things I've never said to you before
but somehow it feels
I must have;
what strange confusion!

I swear I'm not absent-minded
or inattentive;
I have become only
a little forgetful
in your love.

the strange poet

That poet, you know
the one who was so quiet
so strange

He placed his eyes on his ears;
and listened to
the sounds
of mute silences.
He would collect shadows of the moon
drops of dew
scoop dry leaves
and crunch them in his fist.

In the dark jungle
of Time
he plucked moments
raw ones
ripe ones.

Yes, that strange poet
who at night

dragged himself on his elbows
to kiss the chin

of the moon,
fell from the moon last night
and died.

They say, he committed suicide.

the painted sun

Night was in a deep sleep
when I mixed fire and light
and on a white virgin canvas
I painted a sun;
a red, blazing sun.

By morning
the sun had burnt a gaping hole
in my canvas
and there were ashes
all over my room.

a get-together

Death is thick in the air.
Phones
of the city
come together
in a collage.

A sahib says tearfully:
See his face
looks as if he is only sleeping;
seems like if I call him
he will wake up.

Some responsible people
speak with responsibility
"What time will the body be lifted?"
"Get some stale curd"
"Tell them to see his face for the last time"
"Wait for another flight from Delhi,
some people might come."

A car has stopped outside.
All the faces turn;
the wailing which had died down
rises again.

Must be someone important,
someone leaps forward

to hold his hand.

Have strength, have courage
everyone has to go one day.
Who can stop Death?
Have strength, have courage.

Stifling hiccups, the newly arrived
asks between sobs,
"When did it happen? How?
Yesterday he was fine.
Last Tuesday I met him
jokingly he had said:
'If you don't come home this time
I'll never see your face,'"
and broke down again.

Have strength, have courage.

Death is getting stale.
Take him away now;
the talk of death
is congealed in the crowd

"Who was he?"
"Whose body is it?"

"I heard it on the way,
I came right away."
"What happened about your case
in the court?"
"They have postponed it
again."
"I was stunned;
he was healthy, touch wood."
"Place some wood on top of the body."

They have returned.
They have bathed.
It's all over, they sigh.

By evening the ashes will cool down.
The sweeper
will collect the ashes
and the two rupees.

From dust to dust
Tomorrow, in the calendar
when the sun comes up
I won't be there.
I who was "am" will be
"was".

locked silence

Windows closed
chests of walls frozen
the doors have turned their backs
the table, the chair are, like
lumps of silence

Under the floor are buried
noises of the day;
there are locks
on everything
on every lock
a stony silence.

If I can get just a sound
only the sound
of your voice
the night can be saved.
Together
We can save the night.

wooden night

There is no spark
in my body;
from my neck
hang
chokers of broken breath,
bubbles of water
lie paralyzed
in my blood;
sleep sits like a stone,
on my eyes,
The wooden night
lies in my arms
lifeless;
there is no spark
in my body.

It must have been a barren woman
who gave birth to me.

survey

The tremors of breath
do not go away
the wounds of eyes
do not heal
the heart rips apart
every thread of pain.

My soul
has stifled a scream
clenched
between its teeth
my sighs,

you sent a friend
to examine the wounds
on my body;
but who will scrutinize
the wounds of my soul?

come, let's make a poem

Come, let's make a poem.
Let's rake up some wound
and cry.
Let's cut up a vein
or let's just stand
on forgotten crossroads
and call out someone's name;
come, let's make a poem.

my shadow

We are
these days,
estranged,
my shadow and I.

He accused me
of walking in the dark.
He alleged
I walked in the dark
in order to efface him
so he wouldn't track me.
I protested.

I walked alone even in the light,
and in the dark
when I really needed him
he abandoned me.
He took off
leaving no trace—
my shadow, my partner.

We are
these days,
estranged,
my shadow and I.

you

Where have you hidden the night?
Where have you hidden
the touch of your hands?
Where are your lips?
Where are you?
Where are you today?
Why is this silence sleeping
in my bed
tonight?

search

Lost in crevices
like a ray
entangled
in smoke
in dust
I wandered this earth for ages
like a moment
ripped
from Time.

When I found the land
I was lost in the streets.
On the streets
I looked for the house;
In the house
I looked for you.

Now
in your soul
in your body
I wait;
touch me
hold me
give me birth
so I can
make peace with myself.

splinters

With my teeth
I pick up
the pieces of my self
piece by piece.

Who has the time
to look up
at the horizon?
Time sits on my shoulders
splintering
my life into pieces.

You can't pay back
the debts
of life;
not even with life.

some pages of a diary

Who knows whose diary this is!
It has no name,
no address:
"Your memory is turning
my body blue."
and so it says on another page:
"Sometimes the ink of the night
blackens my face.
No matter how much
I wash it with the waters
of dawn
the stains don't go away;
when you see me
you will notice
I have turned dark
almost black."

Scribbled in a column:
"I didn't turn as dark
in the sun
as I have burnt
in this smouldering night."
Scribbled somewhere else is:
"Do you remember
that winter night

when we made love
under an upturned boat?
I wish you were here;
this stony bed would never feel so hard
if wet strands of your hair
were on my pillow
I would spread you like a sheet,
wrap you around like a blanket."

He must have come to the city
for employment:
"I fit in the machine of this city
like a cap on a bottle,
a small
but an essential part.
My chief checks me everyday,
everyday
when another bolt
is tightened on my nerves,
I feel like running away
far away
towards the poisoned horizon."

battle

Fresh blood
from
the wounded sun
stains the horizon
drips on the shore.
Last rays
comb the sand.

Frightened shadows
have fled away.

In a little while
the moon will rise
and declare
the victory
of the night

Once again
I have lost
this day.

unconcluded

On a white bed
lies a body
dead,
abandoned,
a forsaken body
they forgot to bury.
They left
as if death was not
their
business.
I hope they come back,
look
and recognize;

bury me
so I can breathe.

all night, cold winds raged

All night, the cold winds raged;
all night we made love.

I cut some dead branches from the past; you too
plucked leaves of times gone by.
I emptied my pockets
of all dried up poems;
you too took out shriveled up letters.
I threw away the stale lines
of my palms,
you shed all moisture
from your eyelids.

Whatever we found growing
on our bodies
we chopped it
and fed it to the fire.

All night we kept the flames alive
we fuelled the fires of our bodies;
all night we heated a love
gone cold.

desire

My body burns
to touch you.
A hand rises
to stroke your flame;
breath
like a thread
stretches
itself to death.

An empty search.
My arms collapse
and everytime
in my emptiness
I have thought
of passing this void
onto your lap
adding one more flame
to the fires of the soul.

death

Who knows
when or
where
it will strike.
I am afraid
of Life.
Death is okay;
it will strike
only once.

fragile dreams

Look, walk slowly.
Wait,
even slower.
Step carefully, please,
noiselessly;
see that your feet make no sound.

The glass of my dreams
will shatter
and wake me up.

balloon

The swollen rounded sun
like a bloated, tired balloon
is resting precariously
on a bubble
balancing
on a magician's finger.
Blow it and it will vanish
in the water.

It will burst like a balloon,
and once more
one more
burning, scathing, searing day
will vanish.

night

You once gathered it
in your arms.
You let it burrow
in your arms and breasts;
you told long stories
and lullabied it to sleep.
You spoilt it so much.

Today
it is lying on my bed
sobbing.

tonight

Smoke rises from the moon again
tonight.
I will burn in the fragrance again
tonight,
my breath is entangled again
tonight.
It will burst and break.
Your thoughts will not let me sleep again
tonight,
smoke rises from the moon again
tonight.

time capsule

I have wandered through this land of ruins
for so long;

dirty epitaphs
on broken graves
of nights gone by.

Days are torn
asunder
Their crosses lie on the ground;

ashes arise
from the horizon's
cold cremations.

Here, there
everywhere
time is beheaded,
centuries have collapsed.

I have wandered through this land of ruins
for so long
nails have drilled holes
in pure and bloody palms,
blood drips,
bodies of virgin souls
have wasted away,

henna has leaked
from the hands.
The flames rusted,
the lights have faded away.

Blank pages
of blank faces
are open
but the letters of the eyes
have been effaced away.

But
this drop of dew
is eternal
is awake;
it has hope in its eyes,

it trembles
searching
waiting.

The meaning of life quivered
and dropped.
It dropped and is lost.
And I have been wandering through this land of
ruins
for so long.

lovemaking

Cold clouds
on the crimson horizon
drip
in the water;
I sink
in your arms.
I have a faint feeling
that hundreds of bodies
have been lifted from my body

as if the weight of the body
has been eased from the soul.

sun

Round
high
very high, even higher
on a metallic horizon
hangs
this ball of fire.
It must burn for centuries
to melt a drop,
one drop of fire.

When this drop falls
in the void
an echo arises
a moment falls
ripped from time,
a moment
charred with fire
burning, melting
a scalding, scorching moment,
an ashen moment.

prisoner

The dusky evening was sluggish,
tired.
The whole atmosphere was stale
when I entered the city.

Every branch had solitude
clinging to it.
Every wall was branded with silence.

On the roads
there was
no sound
no shadow.

In the streets
there was
no darkness
no light.

All the doors were closed;
the windows
empty.

Only the stale scraps of time
lay around.

I wandered through the city alone
knocking on doors, asking
"Is anybody there?"
I stopped at every crossing.
Maybe someone would come
but no sound
no shadow came.

And then suddenly
the city awoke

the sounds took me prisoner;

sounds roared
sounds screamed.
Every crossing had a mob of sounds
waiting.

In the city of sounds
I remain a prisoner.
My own sounds
have closed on me.

And the road
that led me to this city—
Now even I have forgotten.

a fairy-tale night

Last night
the dew fell
softly
softly;
it fell on the closed lips
of the petals;

Under the veiled night
the fairies
unfurled
the wings of the tales;

In the dull murmuring of the heart
two souls swam
as if weighing the sky
on their delicate wings.

Last night
was beautiful.
Last night
my dreams were alive.
Last night
I was with you.

one night in siddhartha's life

Not a leaf stirs;
there is no movement in the curtains
yet the rapid winds
resound in my ears.

How high are the mirages of the castle!
Higher than the mirages in the star-studded
horizon.
How short I am
like a comma dropped from a word.

Let this mind be stilled
a mind pulled in hundreds of directions.
The hooves of the horses
pulsate in my heartbeat.

Will there be darkness
if the lights are turned off?
Only the eyes will not see the light.
I can plug my ears
but the hissing of the snakes
will not cease;
this light will not leave my being.
Suicide is a darkness
not a solution.

The windows are all open
but why doesn't the air come in?
Outside the window
the two guards are feeding
dried
dead branches
into the fire.

Eyes cannot drop
that skeletal framework.
It was all body
where was the soul?
Was it leprosy,
sickness,
or just old age?
From the chariot I saw
his bones
like dried, dead branches
crushed under
the hooves of time.

Was it suicide,
surrender,
or just an accident?
What was it?

The trees in blossom
render fruits
but when they dry up
they are chopped
and fed into the fire.

Outside the window
the two guards
since evening
have been feeding
dried
dead branches
into the fire.

stranger

I have become a stranger in my own house.

My soul is frightened of me,
my desires shrink from me
and hide in corners,
my longings have turned
out their lights,
my dreams don't recognize me,

my prayers put their heads
on the threshold
and died
on my doorstep.

What land did I seek
outside this house
that I have become a stranger
in my own house?

light

Stars in the sky,
sparks in the eyes,
greasy patches of light
stain my vision.
The pointed light
pokes my eyelids,
hurts my eyes.

Lead me and put me back
in the lap of velvety darkness;
compress the gauze
of pitch darkness
on my eyes:

This burning lava of light
is blinding me.

the poet

Sitting on the mulberry tree
weaving the silken threads,
unfolding every moment,
combing every leaf,
rattling every breath
in his cage,
wraps around him
every unfolded moment;

a prisoner of his own breath,
this poet
will strangle himself with threads
and choke himself
to death
one day.

show

Drop the curtain
the show is over;
drop the curtain
because beautiful sad faces
have disappeared;
each tear has been sucked
from the eyes;
every sound has deserted
the song.

Only the silence resounds,
only the darkness burns.

nights of mourning

Tiptoeing away from me,
silent
without tears
without laughter

a blue glass dome
far away,
the moon
stirs
the dust of silence

once,
only once,
I wish you would wake up
to see what happens
in the nights of separation,
what happens
in the nights of mourning.

poem

A poem
entangled in my chest,
lines
fastened on my lips,
words
like butterflies
won't sit still on paper.

I sit
for so long
with your name
on this blank paper.

Your name
just your name exists;
could there be
a better poem?

wet

In one tune
one rhythm
look, look, how the rain falls.
The entire weather is dripping,
the whole Universe is wet.

Everything is soaked
everything is heavier

From the wet thoughts
in the brain
to the soaking wet
memories;
drip drop
drip drop

only the slow fire of my breath
in my tired body
burns.

am i?

Before the creation of the Universe
the scientists say
there was only
one ball of matter
and nothing else.

There was nothing,
nothing
except God
and God was bored.

There was no sound
no motion
no movement
only a God
lonely
alone a useless God
and the indestructible matter.

The scientists say
in that matter
were
volcanoes,
clouds of gases
fire
mountains

oceans
water
and even air
as if all these elements
were trapped in a body
for millions and millions of years.

Where there was God
there was Space
there was nothing else,
nothing.
Bored
by the centuries of silence
stretching from a long deep sleep,
kicking the matter
he must have said,
"Let there be some movement,
some noise, for God's sake!"

Matter burst
the scientists say,
into little tiny pieces.
These pieces fell
hundreds and millions of light years away
in boundless galaxies

One such piece
away from the centre of the Universe
still burns
everyday.

In our little galaxy
also fell seven, eight, nine balls
of dust
one such lump is the puny Earth
that revolves around its sun
at the speed of sixty-six thousand miles per hour;
so the scientists say.

On this Earth
are oceans, mountains, deserts
and land.
On this land lives a small man
who makes houses out of mud and cement,
breathes,
eats, walks,
even goes to sleep
when he happens to lie down.
Inside his body
is a mind
a mind,

when touched,
questioned,
explored,
discovers the whole Universe.
Does God live there?
Why don't the scientists tell us that?

imprints

Erase all the imprints
of your existence;
move
but make no sound;
don't disturb
the universe of the leaves.
Take off every thread
from your body.
Take off every thread
thread by thread.
Take it off ever so carefully
that you don't touch anything.

Now you are here
Now you are not.

Remember not to disfigure
the face of death
with any wrinkle of life.

taunts

Taunts
of a naïve friend,
like acid
burn my breath,
blister my soul.
"Why shouldn't pain agree with him
it made him rich"—

what should
one do
with such people?
They take a bite
of the golden flower
(searching for gold—)

And fragrance—
it's not for them.

out of order

Who knows what is stuck
what is jammed?
This night won't close,
this day won't open.

hunt

The day has stretched
into evening.
What a runaround
this deer has given me!

A number of arrows
have missed his neck.
He is now as clever
as I am sly.

He provides me with a glimpse
and disappears among the trees
when I reach the trees,
I see him near the falls.
I survey him, keep an eye on him
he too eyes me,
sizes me up.

I wonder who's the hunter
and who the hunted.
When I came to the jungle today
I was sure
I would have
the head of this deer
to wave like a flag
when I enter the city.

The day is running out,
a fear is gripping me;
this deer will lift me on his horns,
take me captive
and drag me to his cave.

broken piece

A broken piece of a poem
drifting in my breath,

When it came up to my lips
it cut my tongue.
When I held it by the teeth
my lips began to bleed
as if a piece of glass
was stuck in my throat.
I could not spit it out;
I was unable to swallow it.

That broken piece of a poem
kept drifting in my breath,
kept drifting,
drifting.

burden

When my shoulders are bent,
saddled
with burdens
of life;
when I am tired,
 so tired
(And when) I think, now—that now
my knees will give in,
a small little poem comes
and stands in front of me
holds my hand and says:
Give me your burden,
come, give it to me,
my poet.

riots

All day I stay soaked in blood.
This blood slowly dries
and begins to darken.
A crust begins to form
which I peel with my nails.
Even the skin begins to come off
with the scabs,
raw odour of blood in the nose,
dark
dried stains on my clothes.

Everyday I get my newspaper
drenched in blood.

a touch of blood

Had this back been a little bit naked
these clothes somewhat tattered
these lips athirst
this stomach resounding with hunger,

Had you peeled
the dried crust on the lips
and left a trace of blood,

Had there been a touch of blood
then this painting
would have been sold
for sure.

scribbles

No, don't erase them.
Let these lines be.
The pink little hands
of my baby
drew these lines,
crooked little lines.

So what if she could not draw a face?
I see her in these lines
I see myself in these lines.

crossroads

Standing at a crossroads
I look at all the roads

one is sluggish;
it drags its feet;
another staggers into a desert;
one is reluctant;
unwillingly it leads
to the cold valley of Death.
The one that goes through the jungle
is frayed, peeling;
yet another jumps blindly into a void.

Standing at the crossroads
I look at all the roads.
Roads, roads,
everywhere.

One day
maybe, one day
you will come
and point to me;
this is the road
this is where we have to go.

the old river

The old river grumbles, Bur Bur Bur Bur
constantly complaining;

what do you care
what people do on your banks?
Don't listen.
Why do you even bother
if that goddamned Madho
lies to his woman?
Let her drown.

You grieve because the midwife
gave you her umbilical cord
when she was born.
Tomorrow when her stomach shows
and she drowns herself,
you will have to hide her body,
for the villagers will only
soil her reputation,
do dirt on her soul.

the old river 2

The old river grumbles, Bur Bur Bur Bur
constantly complaining;
I have seen him spread his legs,
snore all day.
I threw stones
pulled his legs;
indifferent even to the beaks of the seagulls

He is startled
by the raindrops poking his stomach,
his hands helplessly clutch the sands.

the old river 3

The old river grumbles, Bur Bur Bur Bur
constantly complaining;

the waters of his stomach are slowly drying up.
The frail old river
is now hanging
precariously from the cliff
it used to jump from.

Says the cliff to the next stone:
"Take this old man by the hand
take him by the hand
and take him across."

absence

Beyond glass doors,
between thick branches of trees
in spring,
the rain falls, quietly.

There are noises,
there are people;
they are talking.

Beyond the noises of their talking,
somewhere within me,
on another surface
falls your absence, quietly,
very quietly.

faces

In the naked, shameless day
all day long
I whip my slaves.
I buy them,
I sell them,
I auction myself
to satisfy my needs.

In the naked, shameless day
I make deals,
I compromise.

But in the emptiness
of the night
I hide my face
and sob.
One face covers
so many faces.

soul

Entangled
in the wheels of time
these culprits—
souls—
are pulverised on earth.
But everytime
they rise,
only to be crushed again,
something
pulls them back into bodies.

Bodies are crushed,
splintered;
bodies fade away.
Only this soul is not erased
only this soul is not erasable.

evening

Day abandons it
Night disowns it

a poet picks it up
threads it
into a poem;
but sometimes
it is barren,
so impotent
it gives nothing,
not even to the poet.

quest

The sun flung acid in my eyes
sounds pierced my ears
the winds stole lines from my forehead
and fled;

strange hands grabbed my nerves and
Time hammered nails on my hands.

Never again will I search
for myself
outside my loneliness;
never again
will I leave this void.

Not if I can help it,
not if I can help it.

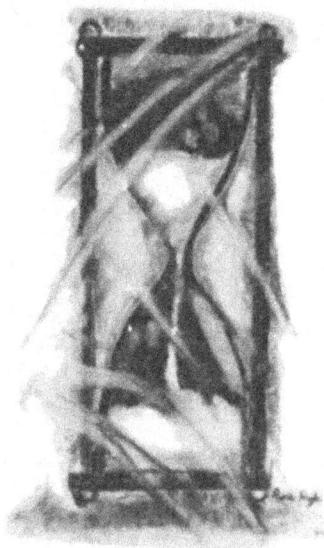

habit

Breathing is a habit
living a ritual.

There is no sound in the body
no shadow in the eyes.

My feet are tired
yet I keep on walking
on this road
an endless journey.

For years
for centuries
we have been living.

We go on living
we go on living.

Habits are so strange.

life

Death comes to everyone
one by one;
why doesn't Life?

captive

When evening comes
shadows fall from the trees,
darkness creeps
on the walls.

I cross an empty jungle
running out of breath
everyday.

I come near this house
and ask—Is anyone there?

Everyday
I go back in vain
but someday
I feel, some sound
some shadow
I hope
will peep
and recognize
and take me away
from this abandoned house
in which I've been locked
for years
and years
and years.

solace

Rip up the entire colony,
gather the roads
wrap up the streets
plunder this city
for no one can make homes
out of bricks and cement.

If the soul finds solace
in the touch of someone's hand then make your
home
there.
Home is
where solace is.

I see the lines of my fate
in your hand.

quiet death

How soundlessly some people die here
dead in the cold graves
of their own rotting bodies!

There is no sound
no sob
no sigh
not even a movement.
How silently some people die here!

You don't have to exert yourself,
you don't even have to bother
to bury them.

note

Same tune,
same note,
the same voice;
yes, the same colour—
even the fragrance is the same.

Drops of dew
lace the branches;
the morning still leaves
footprints
on the leaves.

Along with the notes of sound
is another note.
From your voice
hangs
this note
of silence.

lovers

1 was also in the hall
where the actors on screen
looked so handsome;
everything they said was
larger than life:
their thoughts
their actions;
every action
was a paradigm
for people to see.

I was the actor,
you were the actress;
you held the hands of your lover
and in one eyeful
surrendered your heart.

How real were they—
those actors,
and fake
those shadows
sitting in the hall.

skeleton

The whole body rattles
as if hollow bamboo sticks
are tied together
with a rope.

If that rope unties
the joints, it will
break the connection
scatter the skeleton
and set the soul free
from the body.

This body,
my soul mistook
for a flute;
it slipped in
maybe
to find a note.

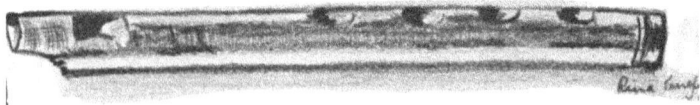

grief

Grief in my heart
has come to stay
as the frightened shadows
of the evening
stop in the jungle
and look back at lonely roads;
the fading lights
stretch the dust
over a distance.

for biba

Cast these sighs away
for snakes live
in sighs like these;
one such sigh
killed Cleopatra.

Place your lips on mine
and breathe all the sighs.
I am immune to poison.

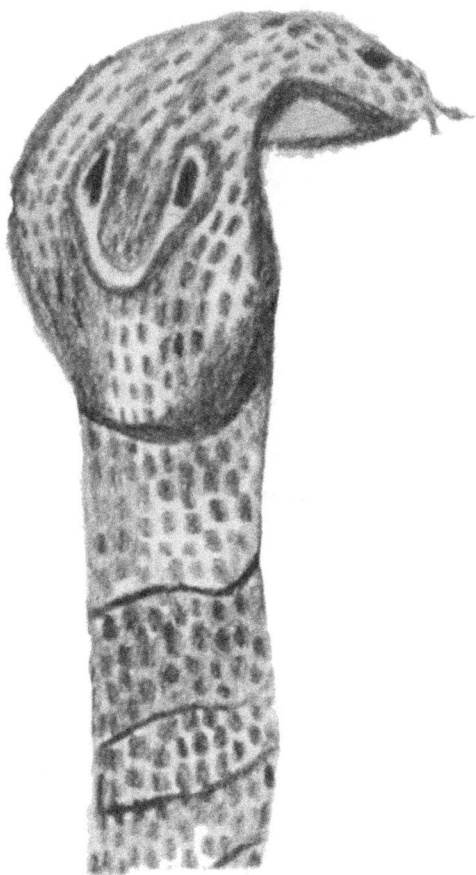

the inherited house

I have inherited an old, frail house
in a toppled valley;

the dry scabs of paint
are falling from
the wounded walls;
the foundations are tired
of standing on one foot.

The bricks are loose teeth
in my jaws,
sprained windows
with dirty, sullied glass
stand at an angle.
Earlier it could open from outside
on squalor;
now shut tight
the suffocated winds
carry holes.

I was born in this house
I have to live here now.

I am afraid
the dirty horizon
on my head
will collapse on me
while I am sleeping,
one day.

van gogh: one more letter

Lumps of sunlight
tempered in turpentine
I spread on my canvas.

What should I do
if they don't see the colours
in my sun?

I should serve the Church,
says Theo to me.
Church,
that Church
where nights are mistaken
for shadows
days are a journey of mirages.

Those who don't understand reality
say my paintings are not real
they are a figment of my imagination.

Let them see the outline of my tree—
Is it less divine
than the tree of God?
God ordered a seed to grow;
it grew.
See how it grew!
When a branch droops,

a leaf falls.
the colours pale,
without any interference
from the artist.

I have worked on every branch,
every leaf;
the eye sees
what the heart sees,
the hand draws.
Just look at the contours of those trees
how upright they are
but none so proud.

See how the leaves shine like copper
in the Fall.

Charred faces
of the "Coal Miners"
damned in the mines.

Let them see the "Potato Eaters"
under the lamplight
taking their meals;
bodies bound together
by the halo.

I saw the wind
flee from the fields,
I arrested it on my canvas.

Roulin,
a schoolboy,

A whore.
A neighbour.
Mortals.
I have immortalized them.

For years I have painted
but my critics said nothing
nothing at all.
Their silence rings in my ears.
Crows' wings
beating against my ears.
My brushstrokes
slashing at their beaks.
I have cut off my ear.
I don't have even a yard
of canvas left
to make a pure sweeping sky
for the sun I prepared

carefully diluted in turpentine.
The sunshine has dried
on my palette.

I am in Remi
admitted in St Remi Clinic
for some repair.
Some parts of my brain
don't seem satisfactory to them.
They say they are disordered,
maybe loose.
I think they are only
a little frenzied.

day

Choking with dust,
battered,
bruised,
defeated,
clinging to the body,
confused,
breathless,
crumpled,
fading away,
running,
panicking,
beating its head against walls—this day.

Before the night comes
I pray it dies
on some cool shore;
for when the night comes,
it will only rake my wounds
again.

naked soul

Thought, breath, vision, pride
give it away, all.
Remove the words
from the lips,
sounds
from the tongue,
peel off the lines
from your palms,
unrobe your body
undress your soul.

Now, give the soul away,
please give it away
Amen!

do not drop the curtain, wait

Do not drop the curtain. Wait,
the tale has not yet ended.

Do not drop the curtain. Wait,
only the bodies have fallen
only the actors have drowned.

The sorrows of the soul still burn;
the pains of the heart still throb;
the feeling is still breathing.

Hold the dying flame.
From this flame will rise another desire
another star will be born
someplace
somewhere

Do not drop the curtain; wait.

geetanjali

The telephone ring
tears apart the sheets of my sleep.
An unknown strange voice
touches me
asks abruptly:
"Are you the poet
who has written all those love poems?"

After a thin shrill silence:
"Write a poem for me too.
Weave me in your verses.
But now—
write it now.
This might be my last night
and this my last wish."

I blow out the phone
and go back to sleep
Now!
Much later
I found out, Anjali,

To fight pain with pain
you sprinkled my poems
on the cancerous fire
of your body.

Whenever I think of that night,
even now,
my eyes fill with smoke.

gulzar

I never thought about my name.
I never really gave it a thought
"Hey, you!" said one
"You there!" said another
suddenly one day you said,
"Gulzar!"

An oyster opened a pearl
I found a meaning.
What a lovely name!
Say it again—
"Gulzar!"

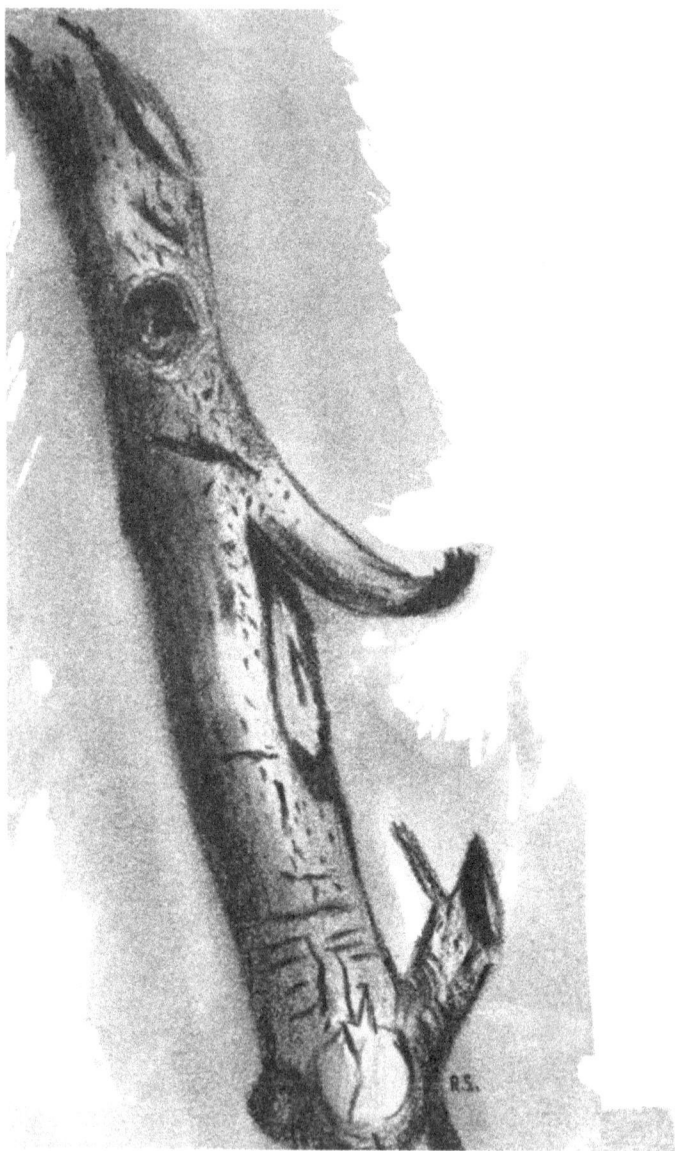

www.ingramcontent.com/pod-product-compliance
Lightning Source LLC
Chambersburg PA
CBHW022153080426
42734CB00006B/421